The truth is, if I am painting I am probably thinking about a conversation
I have had with you.

Written and Illustrated by Kathleen McElwaine

Thank you to all the people who continue to encourage me to share my stories with paint.

My Daddy taught me to seek adventure;
to look for creative solutions;
to always reach out and do my best to help.

I learned this while we cared for the horses, donkeys, cows, dogs, cats, rabbits and QuackQuack, our duck.

He taught me how to ask my friends for forgiveness when I had hurt their feelings.

Seeing the twinkle in my Daddy's eyes when I showed him a drawing of one of the horses was my greatest joy.

I would sketch one of the horses, and when Daddy came home I would ask him to tell me the name of the horse.

He might say any
of our horses' names.

Blue Ribbon,
Eight Bird, Jr.,
V's Lucy,
Mama Molly, or
V's José.

I knew which horse I had
painted. Often it was not the
horse he named.
I would return time and again
to capture those subtleties that
he could see.

Daddy liked to talk about
horse paintings. He might
point to a painting and
say this artist never really
looked at a horse.
This was when I first real-
ized my paintings might
not be just right.

This was an important step
toward becoming an artist,
because I went from child-
like awareness to trying to
draw what I saw.

Sometimes I left the painting unfinished until I could look at the horse to paint it to the
best of my ability.

I cherish the memory of going with Daddy each spring to load the foals in a big trailer and take them to a new pasture, because they had grown so big they needed their own space. Here they met the pasture boss, our donkey. Daddy would open the trailer, and the foals would step out, look around, and see the donkey standing alone in the pasture.

One at a time the foals would run toward the donkey, speeding up on the way. When they reached the donkey, each one would stop and lean on the pasture boss.

We all need to grow up and discover the world on our own...
but it is good to do it in stages.

And then I learned more about donkeys when I started reading the Bible. *

*The ability to paint images inspired by scripture is a gift I hold dear. Two of my favorite scriptures I have illustrated include donkeys: John 12:14, Numbers 22:28-31.

QuackQuack was our pet duck, and the only duck.

My earliest memory with Daddy was walking into the barn with him and seeing our milk cow with her newborn calf.

Watching our milk cow clean her new calf with her tongue was the biggest love I could imagine.

Learning to care for the cows was fun. I learned to tell one cow from another. Daddy taught me how to tell when a new calf was coming. Mama cows would hide their new calves. So, I played hide and seek with the cows each spring.

Most of the time when we arrived at the pasture to feed the cows they would line up, waiting for us, . . .

as if to say "together we stand waiting to be fed".

My love for animals grew as my ability to draw them grew. I became increasingly aware of my surroundings.

I wanted my paintings to tell a story.

Our dog was important. He was allowed in the barn, but not in the house.

One time, when a storm was coming, my sister tried to get our dog into the garage and then into the car with us. He would not get in. Finally we got him inside.
The car smelled like a wet dog from that day forward.

We had cats that lived in the house, and others that lived in the barn. The difference was, the barn cats did not like to be picked up and carried around.

They liked to play with each other. I watched a butterfly play with them. The cats leaped high in the air, but never high enough to catch the teasing insect.

When Doc Brown came to care for the horses he also cared for the barn cats.

It was my job to catch the cats and put them in the tack room for him.

I wanted to raise rabbits. Daddy let me. I found out how many babies they have. I found homes for all the babies when they grew too big to live in the cage with mama rabbit. I learned I did not want to raise rabbits any more.

I loved walking in the woods and spying a wild rabbit. I was happy it was living in the woods and not in a cage.

Mother taught me to find beauty;
beauty in people, and beauty in God's creation.
She taught me to plant good seeds.

I could always find my mom in the garden.

In fact, I suspect that is where she is right now.

Each spring Mother would take us to Binding Stevens Plant Nursery and let us choose 2 packets of seeds to plant in a garden.

I always chose a package of zinnias and . . .

. . . snapdragons.

When Mother described my garden, her words told me what the seeds produced.

But when I told about my garden, this is how I described the flowers.

By June each summer, Quack Quack could be found sitting on a nest of eggs in my garden. Mother and Daddy said the eggs would never hatch, but my sisters and I always hoped we would find a baby duck with Quack Quack some day.

We visited Grandmother on Saturdays, and sometimes after our visit Mother would drive through the neighborhood and tell us stories of her childhood.

Mother often pointed to a tree and told us what she remembered about playing under that tree. Mother always smiled when she talked about trees.

We gave names to trees we knew.

We named this one

The Picnic Tree.

I noticed people smiled at me and spoke nicely when I was busy with my art.

Uncle Bill and Aunt Lillian took me to the museum. I saw artists painting in the gardens.

My sisters loved to go to the library...I did not.

I was 10 years old and still could not read.

When we went to the library, my sisters ventured off to find books. I sat on the floor by the door with my sketch book, drawing what I could see outside.
A crepe myrtle in bloom.

One day the librarian showed me how to find books about artists. I found a big book full of paintings by Rembrandt. I loved every page. I touched pictures of paintings with fabric, thinking they would feel like velvet or leather. I looked intently at the areas of light, wondering where the lamp was sitting.

When I saw that book of Rembrandt van Rijn's paintings, I wanted to learn how to paint!

Painting by Kathleen McElwaine after Rembrandt van Rijn self portrait.

When we came home from the library, I immediately looked in every bookcase. I found a book of Charles Marian Russell paintings. Each page had cursive writing and paintings. I was excited that such an art book existed. I lay down on the floor right then and there. I began painting the pictures in that book into my sketchbook. A short time later I started learning to read. I was convinced that if I could read I would become a better artist because I could read about the wonderful artists I had found.

Daddy told me a story about C.M. Russell. As a young boy, Charlie would lie on the floor, just like I did, and paint pictures of cows, horses, dogs, and people.

Cattle owners noticed how well he could draw and paint. So one day a cattle rancher decided to hire Charlie to ride with drovers on a cattle drive and paint pictures to mail back to him.

In this way, the rancher could understand what happened to the cattle on the way to the sale barn.

Early in Charlie's career as a cattle drive reporter he had painted so many cow skulls that he started signing his name with a cow skull to authenticate that the letter and painting were his own.

A cow skull by Kathleen McElwaine
after C.M Russell.

After I learned to read, Daddy said I was ready for an art class. Jay O'Meilia, a famous artist and friend of Daddy's, taught an adult painting class in his studio on Saturday mornings. Daddy said Jay would teach me. Daddy paid Jay with handmade Nocona Cowboy Boots from our family's store, Dick Bardon Pawn Shop and Sporting Goods.

Jay wanted handmade Nocona boots, and I wanted to learn. It was a good trade.

Jay's Boots

Dick Bardon was a store my Great Uncle Dick Bardon opened in 1902 in Tulsa, during the Oklahoma oil boom years. But that is another story. . . .

"I have the most wonderful life of anybody, EVER".

My quality of life rose to a new level during my years of painting while riding to and from my office at the University of Texas, Austin, on the express bus, and later, on the commuter train. Each day, as I painted, people noticed. They smiled and often asked questions about the process or images. I discovered how important art is to the everyday life we live.

The idea of "Keep The White Space" in your life books came to me during this time of talking about the memory or purpose each painting touched. I wanted to teach anyone who wanted to learn to paint in watercolor. In 2011, I set out to teach my style of art to others. I began to see students' art painted in my own whimsical style. I was encouraged. They often begin to experience joy like I know in their own paintings.

Today I have a studio on the Downtown Square in Georgetown, Texas. I enjoy painting, teaching, and sharing my art in multiple ways every day.

To learn more about "Keep The White Space" in your life please visit:

www.kmcelwaine.com

Kathleen
McElwaine
Art

CPSIA information can be obtained
at www.ICGtesting.com
Printed in the USA
BVHW02s1052250918
527888BV00021B/12/P